Writing
from the
FIRE WITHIN

A Prayer and Writing Workshop

MARGARET MONTREUIL

Other books by Margaret Montreuil:

- *Love's Face* (about Jesus as the Lover of the soul)
- *God in Sandals: When Jesus Walked Among Us* (a novel)
- *God with Us: A Walk Through the Gospels* (devotional companion to *God in Sandals)*
- *His Kingdom Come* (a novel about the primitive church in Jerusalem)
- *The Gardens in God's Story: Avows Divine Romance*

Author Website: www.MargaretMontreuil.com
Contact email: mmontreuil@ymail.com

Cover by Catherine Reishus McLaughlin

ISBN:10: 0-9816845-1-3
ISBN-13: 978-0-9816845-1-2

CONTENTS

ABOUT THIS BOOK

Writing from the Fire Within is designed for Christians seeking the dynamic of prayer and writing. It's perfect for a one-day retreat for those who write-to-inspire, or for individuals who want to experience listening, reflective prayer and journaling.

Structured in five sessions, which normally take one hour each, readers are invited into three movements of prayer and writing: we move inward into personal transformation, upward toward intimacy with God, and outward to minister to others.

Inspiration cannot be forced or manipulated—it comes to us as grace—as do all good gifts from the Creator. In relational prayer we discover God desires to ignite a fire within us, entrusting us with particular inspiration as a beacon of God's fiery love and light.

ABOUT THE AUTHOR

Margaret Montreuil is the author of two New Testament novels: *God in Sandals* is a print, e-book, and an audio book about the life of Jesus; *His Kingdom Come* continues the story and is about the primitive Church in Jerusalem. Her latest book, *The Gardens in God's Story* is about Divine romance. Her first book, *Love's Face,* is about Jesus as the Lover of the soul. Margaret teaches about prayer and facilitates spiritual retreats. She is active in Christian writers groups and mentors others in the art of writing.

Website: www.margaretmontreuil.com
Email: mmontreuil@ymail.com

INTRODUCTION

Welcome to this workshop set apart to be with God focused on prayer and writing. This book is especially designed for Christians who write to inspire and for individuals interested in the dynamic of relational prayer and journaling.

Each of the five sessions end with prayer and writing exercises. You'll need a Bible, notebook, and a dictionary for your prayer experiences. If you are planning a one-day writers retreat or workshop, you'll need to plan about five hours plus additional time for breaks.

Take turns reading the material out loud in the book and designate a "time keeper" for the prayer and writing exercises and for *Session 5 Sharing With Others, Part 2*. Allow at least a half an hour for each of the session exercises unless you see that people are still writing.

Of course, this book can be read independently at one's own pace. If that is the case for you, please take your time and savor it—especially the session exercises.

Your "space" should be free from noise and distractions. If you come to this experience expectant, in faith, God will not disappoint you.

Christian writing has the potential to reach the far corners of the world. Our messages matter because God has lit our hearts with His truth, love, and authority. Let's take this seriously. Let's do as Henry David Thoreau so wisely advised:

W*rite while the heat is in you. The writer who postpones the recording of his thoughts uses an iron which has cooled to burn a hole with. He cannot inflame the minds of his audience."*

If we want to answer the call to write for God, let's take to heart the words the Lord gave to John on the island of Patmos, "Write, therefore, what you have seen, what is now and what will take place later" Revelation 1:18-19.

When we, like John, are "in the Spirit" and are given messages, visions, or inspiration straight from Heaven, let's take his example and write for God.

I hope the ideas presented in this book will not be for one day only but will help equip you to make prayer and writing a lifestyle. When we receive inspiration from our life and relationship with God, who dwells within us, we will write from Divine inner fire.

SESSION ONE

PRAYER AND WRITING

ଔ The Essence of Prayer

Prayer means something different to us depending on our own experiences. Most dictionaries fall far short in describing prayer. Most will include:

1. Act of addressing a divinity; 2. Earnest request.

There are countless books about prayer. One could spend a lifetime and never finish reading them. For one thing, they continue to be written. The last sentence in the Gospel of John says: "And there are also many other things that Jesus did, which if they were written one by one, I suppose that even the world itself could not contain the books that would be written" John 21:25.

John speaks here of the things Jesus did that he witnessed. John couldn't begin to write it all down. Isn't prayer connected with what Jesus continues to do and our witness of it? Every God-inspired book or piece of writing, if it comforts, heals, challenges, teaches, entertains, or helps is a witness of what Jesus is still doing. Prayer is the heart of one's relationship with God.

Here are a few quotes about prayer by people who were intimates of Jesus:

- St. Augustine: "True, whole prayer is nothing but love."
- E. M. Bounds: "Communion alone with God—the Spirit's trysting hours of heavenly love."

9

- Oswald Chambers: "The whole meaning of prayer is that we may know God." He also said: "Prayer is not an exercise, it is the Life."
- O. Hallesby: "To pray is to open our hearts to Jesus. And Jesus is all that we sinners need both for time and eternity."

Prayer remains a mystery to be embraced with faith and love. It is not so much what one does as much as what one experiences.

Richard Foster's book, *Prayer: Finding the Heart's True Home* inspired the ideas I've put together as sessions in this book. (See Credits on Page 61 for more information.) He writes: *"Coming to prayer is like coming home."* That rings true to me. About prayer, Foster says: *"Nothing feels more right, more like what we are created to be and to do."*

Prayer is certainly the heartbeat at the center of our life and our relationship with God, our Creator. Foster says prayer: 1) moves us inward into personal transformation; 2) moves us upward toward intimacy with God; 3) moves us outward to minister to others.

♋ The Art of Writing

What is art, of which writing is but a form? Using a dictionary, you'll see something like this:

> *Art:* 1. Activity of creating things that arouse the emotions through one or more senses. 2. Things so created. 3. Skill of profession as in a skill acquired by experience, study, or observation <the art of making friends>. 4. Cunning.

Good, but insufficient. I'm not content with these descriptions. They are ridiculously incomplete. Madeleine L'Engle had the same trouble trying to define art. In her book, *Walking on Water: Reflections of Faith and Art* she did her homework. She sought to find the best description of what art really is. When she read that art was described as a skill or profession, she said:

> "Is it that? Is a practiced butcher who can skillfully use a knife an artist? Or a dentist's technician? Neither of them would claim to be creating."

L'Engle saw a more personal, intimate perspective in the mystery of being an artist:

> "The artist is a servant who is willing to be a birth-giver. In a very real sense the artist (male or female) should be like Mary who, when the angel told her that she was to bear the Messiah, was obedient to the command. Obedience is an unpopular word nowadays, but the artist must be obedient to the work, whether it is a symphony, a painting, or a story for a small child. I believe that each work of art, whether it is a work of great genius, or something very small, comes to the artist and says, 'Here I am. Enflesh me. Give birth to me.' And the artist either says, 'My soul doth magnify the Lord,' and willingly becomes the bearer of the work, or refuses; but the obedient response is not necessarily a conscious one, and not everyone has the humble, courageous obedience of Mary.'"

Certainly, this is the best way to define the art of writing to inspire. We need to respond to God the same way Mary did when she answered the call to bear Jesus. We need to emulate her response: "I am the Lord's servant, may it be to me as You have said."

Jesus promised to equip us. When He said we would do even greater things than He did, I wonder, do we really believe Him? If His words transformed people while He was Jesus of Nazareth, we can rely on Him, Jesus-in-us, to do the same as He did before, and more.

Inspired writing calls for "walking on water," which is something we cannot do in our own power. However, God anticipates our stepping out in faith to do supernatural things with Him. Peter climbed out from the safety of a boat daring to walk on storm-tossed waves for one reason only: he saw Jesus doing it and thought it would be amazing to do too. And so he called out, "Lord, if it's You, tell me to come to You on the water." After hearing the words "Come!" from Jesus, Peter exercised faith like never before—until he doubted. Just like Peter, there will be times we doubt, fail, or sink. But the main point is that Jesus *wanted* Peter to venture out to do the impossible. In fact, I believe Jesus was thrilled Peter tried it. Remember, Peter stayed afloat and actually did it for a time. Jesus had faith in Peter. God believes in us, knowing we can accomplish the supernatural when we write for Him.

God is always asking us to stretch or do the impossible. That's why faith means so much to Him. Of anything that delights God the most, I'd venture to say it is our faith. Faith produces everything we need to accomplish God's plans and purposes for us.

In art, we become co-creators. An artist, in this case, a writer, sees or hears something (receives revelation) and expresses it—to be noticed, seen, or understood. An artist must listen first and become an open, living stream for the creative waters to flow. Inspiration, using its root meaning, means "God-breathed-in." Jesus promised to fill us to overflowing with Living Water—His Spirit.

Since the very beginning, there has been language—words used to bring meaning to the things of reality, both natural and spiritual. Our words are sounds or a combination of sounds that have meaning, both spoken and written. God's words are more than that: they are creative. Ours can be, too, when they are inspired thoughts.

Once, during prayer, I doubted whether I'd really heard the thoughts of God within me, when the next thing that "occurred" to me was this weighty question: "What do you think thought is?" Of course, I had no answer, but I had my Answer. It's an awesome thing to be with God.

Our word study on art says that the "art of writing" is composing and communicating in an activity of creating something—arousing the emotions through one or more of the senses. Put that together with the meaning of prayer—to communicate with Divinity. Of course, in order to do this, it takes faith.

That word again. Faith. Isn't that what brought you to this workshop on prayer and writing? Imagine Jesus comes and stands before you. He knows everything in your heart. He knows why you want to pray. He knows that you want to write, and He is most likely responsible for putting that desire there. Can you hear the gentle, promising words: "Be it done according to your faith?"

Prayer and writing is simply a way to "hear and record" being with God. Be expectant and attentive, ready to receive. Listen. Believe. Jesus longs for these little talks with you. Jesus delights in times you come to be alone with Him.

Direct words from God can be found in the Bible and they can be found in our own private prayer. Be assured, Jesus will be the center of what happens when you pray during these sessions and let Him say and do whatever He desires. God has invited you into this experience.

It is much like the two disciples when they first saw Jesus by the banks of the Jordan River. They hadn't met Him yet, they had only seen Him from a short distance away when John the Baptist pointed Jesus out to them. They didn't know very much about Him at that point. Eagerly, they ran up behind Jesus and when He turned around He asked them, "What do you want?"

They answered, not knowing what to say and feeling awkward with the need to say something, "Rabbi, where are you staying?"

Surely, Jesus' lips must have parted with a warm smile when He invited them to "Come and see." I believe when we come to Jesus in prayer we will be with Him the same as were John and Andrew.

As a kind of "pump primer" I'd like to share a story from my book, *Love's Face*. In this example of writing to inspire, look for the three movements described in the workshop as:

- Inner Movement: Desire to be with Jesus, open, ready, free, quieting myself in God's presence.
- Upward Movement: Using my imagination to see and experience intimacy with God during meditative prayer.
- The outward expression of that "knowing" in written form in order to show it to others—as "John" described.

A story . . .

When Jesus said "Follow me," He wasn't fooling. You see, all of Israel was waiting for Him. We didn't know it was Him in particular we were waiting for until later. I remember the day I met Him. I set off to follow Him as He walked away from the Jordan River. When I caught up to Him, He turned and asked me what I wanted. Oh, I didn't tell Him then that He was everything Good I ever wanted. Well, I didn't really know it yet myself. I answered by stammering a question about where He was staying. It was my way of following Him without being asked to. I really wanted to be with Him. Andrew was with me and we knew we'd found someone we wanted to know.

Jesus drew me to Himself like a mother hen gathers her

chicks under her wing—I belonged to Him somehow. And always will. He knows what we all really want—to follow Him. Come to think of it, in following Jesus one never stays in the same place for very long, do they? Spiritually, I mean.

Well, having a famous friend was exciting. People were so drawn to Him. We just couldn't help ourselves. The miracles were phenomenal. Every town, village, and roadway buzzed with stories. His words were quoted everywhere He went. But who could believe such fantastic things? You had to hear Him firsthand to have a chance at believing. And, of course, everyone in Israel had his own opinion. We Jews are known for that. And, let me tell you, Jesus had no qualms about stating His opinions. Some of the things He said were hard and tested a person's motives and heart to the quick. He had an uncanny way of reading people. He knew things about them that showed in the way He looked at them, or how He touched them, or by what He'd do for them. He was untiring in love and patience. But, sometimes, He'd be so sharp with someone it would startle me. He knew someone's motives and would, with a single comment, turn his whole hypocritical, self-righteous world upside down. I'd watched Him turn into instant stone with certain people. Other times, a look from Him could cause a melting of one's whole being. His looks of compassion were the most common of all. Sometimes I'd weep just watching Him interact with people. His love was powerful.

I saw plenty of His enemies stomp away from Him in anger. The religious leaders especially despised Him. One thing they loathed was how the sinners came to Jesus, spent time with Him, and listened to Him. I think at first they thought Jesus was a man of compromise, willing to be a sinner like those with whom He kept company. But then when so many known sinners started appearing in the synagogues and temple to pray and worship, the scribes and teachers of the law became jealous. How did Jesus reach so many sinners? They never could.

I knew how. He did the opposite of what they did. Instead of snubbing people and pointing a finger, instead of giving them a list of do's and don'ts, instead of telling them how to be right with God, Jesus accepted them and got to know them. He preached very little to His listeners, although He told them many a good story. They couldn't help but like Him. I watched how Jesus' goodness rubbed off on anyone who came close enough to really listen. When they asked for advice or teaching, then He'd give it. And, they asked. I learned a lot from watching Him.

Once He called me a "son of thunder" after I had made a wild comment that He should strike a Samaritan town with lightning from Heaven because they were rude to Him. He shook His head and smiled to Himself, and then He called me that name. His humor hinted of a love mixed with patience and loving wisdom that reached far beyond my short-sightedness. I often found myself feeling incredibly foolish, yet under His endearing gaze, completely accepted. He said I didn't know of what spirit I was. Well, I have a better idea now. You see, His Spirit is nothing but love. The closer I got to Him, the more I could see that this was no ordinary relationship I shared with Him. My soul was drawn to Him, I felt beloved of God, favored by Him. I eventually learned about that Spirit of His, of His great love, and that that was the Spirit I belonged to.

The last night we were all together, I rested my head on His chest. There I was the most content I have ever been. I heard His heart beat and felt His warm breath tickle my hair. His low voice soothed me whenever He spoke aloud.

I wondered if he knew my thoughts because He often did.

He whispered my name, "John." My name, sounding from His lips, was love. Oh, my name said so closely and gently. I wanted to stay close forever. I'd do anything for Him.

Incredulous, one friend leaning on Him and another one running out the door, ready to betray Him. I will never understand Judas. There are many Judases, though. I have been like him. We are all so unworthy of Jesus' love, aren't we?

I couldn't grasp Jesus' true identity then. While He walked around most of Israel with me, well, I never prayed to Him when we were apart. I do now. I'm discovering what "Spirit I am of" more and more. Looking back, I can remember Him, but I am closer to Him today than I was then. We talk the same way we used to when I'm praying. I can sense His eyes looking at me with love. I see Him doing things for me. Sometimes, I'll be in the middle of some present task, and suddenly, out of nowhere, comes this sweet sense of His presence and love. It's as though He walked into the room, the same way it was back then.

He was right about knowing Him and worshiping Him in spirit and truth and that He would always be with us. I remember the day He said that. I was so happy after the hellish thing we'd all been through. He was radiant! He was alive and with us again! After He left us physically, I expected to join Him soon. I would welcome death, if that came first, to be able to reunite with Him. Yet, here I am in old age, still waiting. Ah, even the waiting is full of His presence with me.

One day, before He physically left us for Heaven, He made us feel especially loved and hopeful. He assured us of His closeness, no matter what. Well, we believed Him. Not a word of His would be doubted again. I love Him with all of my heart—sometimes so much it hurts. Something I've noticed, that has never changed, is that the more I know Him and experience His love, the more I want. It's so ironic. Often, I used to notice such a pained look on His face when He addressed people. I never understood it until I felt it myself, only now I feel it for Him. My God! My God, you are all I want! Your love is all that matters. Yes, Heaven has come to earth so that we could be in Heaven.

You know, I think I'll write these things down. I have to find some ink and something to write on. The Word of God has come and I have seen and touched Him. And, I still do. Oh, we all can. Come, Lord Jesus. Come, through my words. Come, through your Word. Yes, come, Lord Jesus!

Writing, as a way to pray and reflect, will be our first exercise in this workshop. Enjoy this time set aside to be alone with God in this meeting place of prayer and writing.

❦ A Meditation for Inspiration

"For lo, I am with you always
even to the very end of the age."

Matthew 28:20b

Read the above Scripture verse to yourself slowly a couple of times. Then close your eyes and sit quietly, long enough to feel still and focused within. Allow the verse to settle into your mind and heart then begin the following reflective meditation.

Now read, but go very slowly.

Soon, Jesus would be on His way to Heaven.

He was saying important last words. Words of Goodbye.

Or, was He?

Hear His voice. Notice the particular words He chose.

They are poetic, dramatic, and emotional.

How could these mere words hold all of His meaning?

Somehow, they try to hold His very heart.

And, every time Jesus says something—

the action of it follows at once.

"Let there be light."

"Receive your sight."

"Arise, little girl."

God's words create.

They cause the reality of what He intends.

Jesus had accomplished His mission—to abolish the separation between God and us.

How delighted Jesus must have felt to say:

"I am with you always."

Perhaps Jesus comforted Himself not just His followers.

He had suffered much for the joy set before Him.

How endearing this experience was when He looked into His followers' eyes and said the words. He must have had a great look of love on His face, His eyes pools of love, His voice expressive, full of joy, authority, comfort, and promise.

Jesus' promise for His continued presence includes you and me: "Go therefore and make disciples of all the nations, baptizing them in the name of the Father and of the Son and of the Holy Spirit, teaching them to observe all things that I have commanded you; for, lo, I am with you always, even to the end of the age."

Lord Jesus thought of us when He commissioned His closest followers at one of His favorite places to pray—atop the grassy mount that ascended gradually behind the fishing town of Capernaum. His words would reach the four corners of the globe and to the end of the age.

Did Jesus ever say Goodbye?

"The Kingdom of Heaven is in your heart," He said.

"For lo, I am with you always," He said.

History has defined this meaningful occasion in Galilee when Jesus spoke these words of blessing as "The Great Commission" but it was not the last time Jesus appeared to the disciples nor did He ascend into Heaven at that time. Jesus ascended from the Mount of Olives in the vicinity of Bethany only days before the Feast of Shavuot (Pentecost). He appeared to them many times over a period of 40 days after His resurrection.

On the Feast of Shavuot/Pentecost, the Lord then filled His followers with the Holy Spirit and He continues to do so. Jesus never said Goodbye.

❦ Prayer Journal Exercise for Session One

Close your eyes and experience being in the presence of the Lord. Let His love hold you close. He is here. He is with you always.

Open your journal to the first blank page and include today's date at the top of the page with a notation that this is a prayer and writing exercise. Then, begin.

Write whatever comes to you as you consider the following:

What do you sense God wants to share with you?

If you do not hear anything initially, then reflect on what thoughts came to you from this chapter's Scripture verse or whatever ideas stirred your heart during the meditation about The Great Commission.

We often see that post-resurrection event as a kind of Goodbye on Jesus' part. It wasn't that at all. What was Jesus' intention truly about on that day of The Great Commission?

Listen and pay attention to whatever thoughts come to you.

Record whatever you would like to remember about this time of prayer, reading, and reflection.

SESSION TWO

INNER MOVEMENT—PERSONAL TRANSFORMATION

ଔ God in Us

God comes to us in reality and abides within us. This inner relationship is by faith. The people who saw Jesus in the flesh saw Him outwardly. Even they had to see Him inwardly, through faith, in order to know Him in reality. And, in knowing Jesus they became like Him. He filled them with His Spirit. His anointing was given to them. This anointing was His own to give, it was His authority, power, and truth. That is how it must be with us now.

A Christian is in close relationship with Mystery. We can't fully comprehend the Father, the Son, and the Holy Spirit as One but that's okay. Even so, God wants to be known and embraced by us. We will be changed once we know Him.

Inner transformation begins when Jesus takes central place in our hearts and lives. We become new creations with new hearts, new desires, new direction, and a new frame of reference. As we grow to know God and His ways more and more, we become our real self—the unique individual God is making us to be. We will reflect the likeness of Jesus more and more. Christian means "little Christ" because the Lord Jesus Christ is in us in the form of the Holy Spirit.

Prayer is vital to our relationship with God. However, it is not only asking God for help, or experiencing one-way conversation. Prayer is relational. It can be crying in God's presence, sharing a moment of thanksgiving when it strikes you, noticing when a coincidence has the fingerprints of God all over it. Prayer is not something we do, it is a way of life. We can enjoy unceasing prayer by being aware of God's presence moment-by-moment. From spiritual birth on, we're developing into God's "beloved" and we are unique. He loves us particularly. Knowing God is our "inner life" with Him.

The more we know God the more we will know ourselves. We will meet our "selfish" self which must die consistently as we discover our precious, true identity. We will see ourselves from God's perspective—beloved. We will know God and learn what we mean to Him, why He favors us, what He loves about us, and why we are on earth. This is everything. We discover who we are and what we are meant to do. Living in God's love is how we become our truest selves. Our Creator's love is *for* us always.

⚇ Personal Transformation through Prayer and Writing

Keeping a Prayer Journal. This can help us see or notice God in our lives. It's an easy method of therapeutic self-help, cheaper than counselors. Many people use this method to process, understand, "get something outside that is within" and it has been proven to release stress and burden. It actually can help one to learn and understand. It can be as simple as documented prayers to God. It's a way to talk to God and document what you've shared.

Experiment with styles and methods. You might enjoy scrapbook type journals, word-processing electronic files, 3-ring binders, and spiral notebooks. If the fancy "gift" type journals inhibit you—if you are too concerned you'll mess up the nice book, then don't use them for prayer journaling. You could use them for quotes you love, or for poems.

Some people pray as they write. Some write after they pray. Be honest. Be open. Get down your feelings and thoughts. Write to the Lord. Write about the Lord. Write about your life. Some of your journal pages might include household budgets, income and expenses figured and refigured—because this was your concern at the time. Turn a page, and it's a poem, or a sketch of a lake with swimming ducks. This is a safe place to write down what God is speaking, sermon notes, quotes from books you are reading. God meets us in our faith.

Include the date so that when you periodically review your entries, you'll be able to see answered prayers, patterns, and reminders. You'll be able to look back and see how God has been with you in the past. You'll be reminded of the miracles and joys in life when you are feeling down or spiritually dry. Watch for cycles, rhythms, and spiritual growth—you'll be reminded of things God has told you or things you've learned. Sometimes your journal can help you make decisions or sort things out. It can be helpful for discernment.

Prayer journaling is more than getting out what is inside written down. It can become conversation because someone really is listening and that Someone is God. That Someone can and will do something about what we share with Him. If we can focus on God in our prayer—as we desire and seek His face—we will come to know Him in deeper ways.

When we combine the method of writing with prayer an incredible phenomenon occurs—truth is revealed. We will encounter Truth. Jesus, the true Light, will come, dispelling darkness as He does so. When we come to the Lord in prayer in the darkness of faith and with honesty and authenticity, God meets with us and gives revelation and illumination. Jesus promises to manifest Himself to those who seek Him with all of their heart. An amazing thing happens when we pray and seek God's face, we will better see ourselves from God's perspective.

We've already covered this aspect of transformational prayer but it is worth repeating. We will discover our real self, the person God is creating us to be when we experience His particular love. This self-knowledge leads us to enjoy who we are, not in pride, but in a way that draws life from God's love and acceptance.

We will hear our own name, perhaps an endearing nickname that is our own, spoken from His heart. We find out who we are from the One who made us. We can find meaning and purpose in life.

Writing as a Way to Process and Remember. Besides keeping personal journals, people write letters (some they never send), books, autobiographies, memoirs, letters, even internet blogs to process the happenings in life.

It's possible to find direction, to be healed from past wounds or experiences, to learn and discover, all this and more, through the creative experience of writing. A good example is the book and movie: *A River Runs Through It.* The author, Norman Maclean, wrote his story to process the dramatic, tragic events that had happened in his family. He said, "There was no clear line between religion and fly fishing."

One critic said, "It is the truest story I ever read; it might be the best written. And to this day it won't leave me alone." Maclean never intended to publish his story, he wrote it for himself.

Think of what Anne Frank's childlike journal has meant to so many people and nations. Through writing, God can heal us and others.

Keep Moving. Journaling and processing our concerns and issues too much can cause an overt amount of introspection. This can cut off our ability to encounter God. Self-examination and confession of sin is good, to a point. We must not allow our spirituality to become like a pool of stagnant water which sits in its own elements. The living water of our experience with the Spirit of God is full of movement. We move inward to find that quiet, expectant place of faith. God can be found inside of us there, in the center of our being, in our heart, through our faith. There we need to be still, be quiet, be open, and listen. If all we think and care about during prayer is ourselves, our own problems, needs or desires, we can become stuck—and sink in the mire of self-centeredness. That is why when we pray we should look at Jesus, and focus on that sweet Character, on God's beauty and goodness. Sometimes, all our worries, needs, and aspirations for family, profession, ministry, whatever it is, can cause us to spin around and around in self, and never reach the heights of life centered in God, for which we were created. We were made to enjoy and know God. Why do we settle for so much less, for self-interest, for misery and want? Love God with your entire heart, mind, and strength and all will be well!

Above All, Prayer is Love. Whatever brings us closer to God is well worth the effort. Prayer and writing has that power.

Our faith is meant to be a Divine love affair. It is from that central fire within that we move and have our being.

ଔ Prayer Journal Exercise for Session Two

The following four suggestions are for prayer and writing. Choose one from these four exercises that most appeals to you. Be sensitive to what seems to stir your heart to do. Not all of these will work for you—don't be concerned at all about why. You may wish to do more than one of them if you have time. Read all of them first and then choose.

Try not to feel rushed during this time of prayer and writing.

1. Think back over your spiritual life, from as far back as you can recall right up to now. Take time to reflect on the highs and lows, the moments of breakthroughs, stagnant times, periods of growth, times of crisis, etc. In your journal, describe the ups and downs with a line drawing or a graph that shows your faith journey. Start at the beginning up to today. Include year markers, if needed, and then show times God showed up. Include life-changing events. This will help you get an overview of how God has been present in your life.

    Or, instead of a line graph, write an outline or a narrative synopsis to describe your faith journey. Include major happenings in your relationship with God and note times when God spoke to you or helped you, times Jesus manifested Himself to you.

    Or, draw pictures that capture your relationship with the Lord in artistic images.

2. Ask God this question and then listen for a response:

    "Lord, what do You love about me?"

3. Imagine the Gospel account of John 1:35-39. This is the occasion when Jesus invited John and Andrew to "Come and see." After reading the Scripture verses, pray with the questions that follow as if Jesus were speaking with you face to face. The

following is paraphrased from John 1:35-39. Note that here we first see red letters in the Gospel: "What do you want?"

> *Again, the next day, John the Baptist stood with two of his disciples and saw Jesus as He walked. "Behold the Lamb of God!" John said.*
>
> *The Baptist's two disciples left him and caught up to Jesus, who turned around and asked, "What do you want?"*
>
> *They replied, "Rabbi, where are You staying?"*
>
> *"Come and see," Jesus said.*
>
> *They came and saw where He was staying and remained with Him the rest of the day.*

Can you see Jesus asking you these questions as your focus for prayer and listening? Be open to any other inspiration that comes.

> *What do you want?*
>
> *Why are you doing this workshop?*

4. Use Psalm 131:1-2 as your own prayer:

> *"My heart is not proud, O Lord, my eyes are not haughty; I do not concern myself with great matters or things too wonderful for me. But I have stilled and quieted my soul; like a weaned child with its mother, like a weaned child is my soul within me."*

Become like a weaned child. Let God hold and rock you in His loving arms. A weaned child no longer needs his mother's milk but is mature enough to feed himself. Still, this weaned child craves intimacy and remains dependent.

Stay with this as long as it seems to have life. After you are finished, write in your journal a description of what your meditation was like.

SESSION THREE

UPPER MOVEMENT—INTIMACY WITH GOD

❧ Relational Prayer

Just as in any relationship, stages of closeness and openness develop and change. Prayer journals will reflect the stages of your relationship with the Lord. It may include such things as poetry, letters, keepsakes, musings, drawings, diary-type entries. Your journals and prayer life will change just as will your relationship with God.

The following are normal stages, or phases, typical in any relationship. Remember, prayer is not doing something, it is being with Someone.

- **Stage 1: Casual.** Communication is safe. I stay polite and guarded; I pray for others and myself.

- **Stage 2: Beginning Trust.** We have dialogue about real concerns and issues that matter to me. I speak of what I think and feel. I become more open and vulnerable with the other person. This stage with a prayer journal might begin to look like letters to Jesus, open and honest. I am recording life events and talking about concerns, asking God for direction, wisdom, help. God will be speaking through many channels: Bible verses, sermons, books, friends, life events. All these ways and more might be described in my prayer journal at this stage.

- **Stage 3: Deep Trust.** I share my dreams, mistakes, frustrations, and secrets. I am learning that I am trusted also with God's concerns, feelings, desires, and purposes.

- **Stage 4: Loving Intimacy.** We know each other deeply. We exchange love and affection in many ways. We desire to please each other. We know what the other one will think, say, or feel in most situations. We deeply understand each other's desires and disappointments. We can sit quietly with each other, experiencing each other's presence, without words and beyond words.

- **Stage 5: Union.** We are one. I have become one with the other, comparable to a mature, loving marriage relationship. We become so much a part of each other that we speak, feel, act, and react together.

"Prayer Journaling" or "Two-Way Journaling" are terms for what happens when one records inner dialogue with God.

This is not to say that mental illness and evil spirits can't influence us as well. One must be mindful of this possibility, and the fact that we can imagine God's voice too. But do not let these negative possibilities rob you of the intimacy that can be yours with God. Because it would take us off task for this workshop, I'd like to refer you to an excellent book. *4 Keys to Hearing God's Voice* by Mark and Patti Virkler, published by Destiny Image Publishers.

Here are just three supporting Scriptures for listening to God's voice:

- *"My sheep hear My voice, and I know them, and they follow Me"* John 10:27.

- *"On the last day, that great day of the feast, Jesus stood and cried out, saying, 'If anyone thirsts, let him come to Me and drink. He who believes in Me, as the Scripture has said, out of his heart will flow rivers of living water.' But this He spoke concerning the Spirit, whom those believing in Him would receive; for the Holy Spirit was not yet given, because Jesus was not yet glorified"* John 7:37-39.

- *"I still have many things to say to you, but you cannot bear them now. However, when He, the Spirit of truth, has come, He will guide you into all truth; for He will not speak on His own authority, but whatever He hears He will speak; and He will tell you things to come. He will glorify Me, for He will take of what is Mine and declare it to you. All things that the Father has are Mine. Therefore I said that He will take of Mine and declare it to you"* John 16:12-15.

When we listen in faith, asking God for the Holy Spirit, our Father God will not give us a stone. Faith is the key to receiving God's gifts. Creative ideas will come to us. Ideas and messages from God will inspire and guide us—they may be in visions, a sense of peace, insight, or words.

Consistent study of God's Word will ground you, provide you with discernment and enable the Holy Spirit to personalize what your mind understands. Meditation, reflection, and prayer moves what you learn into your heart and life experience.

An example of listening prayer. *Excerpts from Your Move God* by Francis Clare:

> "To be one with Me means to lose yourself in the heart of your Father so that we are no longer two but just one. My child, for almost two thousand years My Son has been praying for this oneness that you may be one in Me as Jesus is one in Me. I promise you, we will be one.

> "Your life is Our life. I, your Father, watch over it with you. It is not a monstrous task We give you to live Our life. It is Our task to keep your old life dead and to live Our new life. Let Us have it. Enter into that Hebrew rest—pondering—listening—discerning—resting. Allow Us to initiate, to act, to arrange. You have a Husband who would do for you all the

lovely things a good husband would do for a bride. You have a Father who loves you as He loves Jesus. You have a Holy Spirit who has pledged to be your life. You have a family of brothers and sisters cheering for you. You are part of a vast army of Christians who have learned that the only thing worth living for and worth dying for is the Father's love.

The following quote is from a 365-day devotional book taken from *Jesus Calling* by Sarah Young, Copyright © 2004. Used by permission of Thomas Nelson. www.thomasnelson.com. This powerful little book proves how much people long to hear the Lord in dialogue prayer. This book has remained at the top of the Best Seller Christian Book List for years. Sarah Young's devotional ideas put into the first-person voice of Jesus is powerful. It was first published in 2004 because this prayer listener, Sarah Young, believed in dialogue prayer and shared her journal ideas with others.

"I AM WITH YOU. *I am with you. I am with you.* Heaven's bells continually peal with that promise of My Presence. Some people never hear those bells because their minds are earthbound and their hearts are closed to Me. Others hear the bells only once or twice in their lifetimes, in rare moments of seeking Me above all else. My desire is that My 'sheep' hear my voice continually, for I am the ever-present Shepherd.

Quietness is the classroom where you learn to hear My voice. Beginners need a quiet place in order to still their minds. As you advance in this discipline, you gradually learn to carry the stillness with you wherever you go. When you step back into the mainstream of life, strain to hear those glorious bells: *I am with you. I am with you. I am with you.*"

(This is the daily devotional for October 30.)

I meet the Lord with my prayer journal. I sit expectantly still and quiet with pen in hand. Whenever I read Scripture I pay attention to what stirs my heart. This becomes a personal "living" word from God's "written" word. God meets me in this place of desire and faith. God desires "communion"—being in relationship with us more than we do. He delights to see our faith.

I talk with God—my thoughts and His intermingling—my love and His intermingling. Whatever is happening in my life finds its way in my prayer journal. A bonus is that I can keep the journals and revisit my times with God. It is like a stack of love letters to and from my Beloved. It is like a travel log of my journey in faith, in God's kingdom of love. I've kept prayer journals for over thirty years. It is incredible to see how I have changed, as well as my relationship with the Lord. It is wonderful to keep track of how God faithfully walks with me in all of life—sometimes a savior, or a teacher and counselor, sometimes a father, often an intimate friend—and most graciously and mysteriously, as the Lover of my soul.

I'd like to share a true story about what happened with the Lord and me, a long time ago, but the memory is still vivid and wonderful. I discovered how much Jesus delights in my prayer journal.

A testimony . . .

A friend of mine was leaving to visit Israel and would spend a few days in Jerusalem. She agreed to deliver gifts for me to a family I knew who lived there.

Valentine's Day was coming up. Another thing going on was that I had taught my Sunday school 4th through 6th graders how to write a "Psalm" to God. We were studying King David and we were reading some of his Psalms to God. During class, I asked them to write a Valentine to God, one that meant how they really felt. That was my way of teaching them what the Psalms were like on their own level.

I came up with the idea to write a Valentine Psalm to Jesus and ask my friend to stick it in the Western Wall near the Temple mount in Jerusalem for me. This is a revered place where visitors to the Western Wall, also called the Wailing Wall, come from around the world and stuff prayers into the cracks of the ancient limestone wall.

Think "Valentine boxes" decorated in elementary school. I had this rather whimsical idea to drop my Valentine off in the Messiah's "box" in Jerusalem at the Wailing Wall. (The best address for anything handwritten, right?) It was just a small gesture on my part.

I arrived at my friend's house with the gifts she'd agreed beforehand to take to my Jerusalem friends and then I asked her if she'd also put a prayer note in the Wailing Wall for me. She agreed. I immediately wrote something to the Lord on a scrap piece of paper that was lying on her dining room table. As I folded it, I heard inwardly, "Use your prayer journal paper, will you?" I happened to have my prayer journal in my purse.

I quickly tore about a 5 inch piece out of it towards the back where I knew the paper was unused. I sketched a heart and wrote on it "I love you, Yeshua, and I am longing for You to return here to Jerusalem." My friend took the folded paper and carefully placed it in her purse and later she stuck it in a crack in the Wailing Wall.

Weeks later, while I was prayer journaling, I turned the page of my notebook while writing what was then a continuous flow of Jesus' words to me—coincidentally, He was talking about how He longs to come to Jerusalem to redeem His Bride—and how much He loves the very paper of my journal, and did I appreciate enough yet how sentimental He is? These words that happened to flow around the missing quarter of that page I'd randomly torn out to use for my Valentine.

The tone of His message seemed lighthearted, possibly as whimsical a gesture mine had been. What a sentimental person He is—and how does He pull off these kinds of things? Think of the orchestrated forethought, as well as collaborative effort, on His part.

I thought of all the symbolism and sentimentalism that is so prevalent in the Jewish rituals, the Feasts, the celebrations, of which He instigated. God loves to celebrate anniversaries.

What was incredible to me was that this was such a coincidence that the Lord's words came to me then and there—I was so deeply moved—tears streaked the ink from joy, and my joy was certainly mingled with His. God's words of love had streamed on THE exact missing page in my journal. I'll always treasure that experience.

Understandably, we grow closer to God in our prayer life. God uses our imaginations' inner screens to reveal His image to us. The word image found in the word imagination is because we can receive images from God there. God created us this way. The Holy Spirit uses many forms of images to reveal Himself to us, Story and Creation included. When our reflections and meditations arise within our hearts from God's heart, a wonderful phenomenon occurs: Divine revelation.

When I found myself daydreaming about Jesus—I would imagine being with Him in Gospel stories. I struggled with whether or not it was right or foolish. I told myself, "I should be praying." I felt at the time that intercession and dialogue was prayer. But my longing heart simply wanted to see and be with Jesus. He had given me such a vivid and creative imagination. I had no idea that what my heart desired actually led me on a common spiritual path—for those seeking the face of God. I was drawn through desire into meditative prayer.

A testimony . . .

I often imagined being with Jesus in Gospel accounts. One day, after I had done this, I repented of it to God, thinking it was foolish and wrong to do. I felt like a child who hadn't learned to stop imagining and pretending. After repenting for the imagined experience, my desire for Jesus spurred me on later the same day to go to a Christian book store. I just had to get more of Jesus. I felt that if I read about Him, then my desire would be somewhat quenched.

With my arms full of books, I was on my way to the cashier to pay for them when I sensed the Lord's voice within: "You haven't got the right book." I returned to the shelves and put all the books back. Then I caught sight of one that peaked my interest: *The Joy of Listening to God* by Joyce Huggett. I opened the book to its middle section (the lucky-dip) and began at once to read her teaching about what is classically known as "Divine Reading" or "Sacred Reading." She taught that a person may imaginatively place oneself in a Gospel story with Jesus to see and experience being with Him—it's a form of meditative prayer.

Was my perfect find in the book store a coincidence? No way. That was the book I took home. I determined to follow my love for Jesus because it seemed to be leading me to Him. My desire for Jesus brought me to a new stage of growth in prayer development.

It was while I enjoyed "sanctified imagination" prayer encounters that I fell in love with the Lord more deeply. I have used journaling to document many of my experiences and have grown spiritually from them. I think the most significant part of it has been seeing Jesus' humanity—to see and experience God close up. Listening, pondering, meditation on Scripture, all became part of my experience of God. Love is the reason. Love draws us in and close to God.

Our imaginations were created for God. Why should only self, Satan, or the world be the only ones to show their scenes? Our eyes and ears were made primarily to know God! He certainly wants to use our imaginations—God expresses Himself through *story* and *beauty* and always has. If you are called to write for God, then you will be naturally gifted with a creative imagination and your prayer life and relationship with God will act as fuel for the fire of inspiration.

෪ **Prayer Journal Exercise for Session Three**

Using the following steps of reading, meditation, pondering, and journal writing, we will enjoy a time with God. Pick one from these Scripture suggestions from a Gospel scene while being sensitive to which one most draws you:

- Mark 5:21-34: A woman is healed by touching Jesus' clothes.

- Mark 5:35-43: Raising a young girl from the dead.

- Luke 7:36-50: A woman anoints Jesus' feet.

- John 21:1-24 Jesus appears on the shore to the disciples after His resurrection.

1. **Begin by praying** that the Lord will guide you and be with you during this time of prayer and writing. In faith, be attentive to Him. Read the Scripture slowly, paying attention to the details. If you wish, read before and after the story to get it into the right context.

2. **Reflect/Meditate:** Imagine what you have read by becoming part of the story. Allow it to flow with a life of its own. Suggestions: Imagine being part of the scene. Be a disciple, or someone healed, a fictional character who is there, or imagine you are there—time/space traveling—use your imagination. Use your five senses too. Hear the sounds, smell the smells, feel the wind, etc. Look at Jesus closely, see His expressions and how He seems—His tone of voice, His clothing, the look in His eyes. Listen to His words. Continue until it ends.

3. **Ponder:** Sit quietly, open to God. Simply BE with the Lord. Sometimes there may be more dialogue, a vision, sense of love, faith, joy, peace. Be open to whatever the Lord grants. Complete silence is wonderful too. You are in God's presence. Intimacy in silence is quite special.

4. **Journal Writing:** Document the experience. Often, writing as a way to reflect adds to the experience revealing more than your time of meditation itself. Keep your heart, your inner "ear," open while doing this because God may reveal more as you write. This enriches the experience and you will have it documented to review and remember.

SESSION FOUR

OUTWARD MOVEMENT—WRITING TO INSPIRE

∞ The Ministry of Writing

How do you know if you are meant to be a writer called to inspire others? Well, there are signs of it. First, you'll be a reader and will appreciate words—it's a love and a craft. Second, you'll want to. Third, you'll have some natural talent. Fourth, you'll become a bit driven because it is a lot of work, wrought with disappointment, and difficult to succeed in the competitive, often profit-oriented, publishing industry. Fifth, you will feel strongly that you can't NOT write. Now that sounds like poor English, but it is every bit true.

Other signs might be that stories come to you, characters visit you and want to become real. You may have something bursting to be written down. The most important thing you must know is that you need to write not just for God's behalf, but for yourself, not even so much for an audience or for anyone else. Write what you are excited about even if it is not in the norm. You will have no fire of God to spread to others without the particular passion that's yours.

Prayer will take you there. Your relationship with God will be the driving force to be sure. You are the only one who can write the unique things you are meant to say. You might ask, "Who, me?" It's all right to feel that way. God most often chooses ordinary, non-distinct people to work through. History shows it. Even Jesus Himself was misunderstood because of His ordinariness. He blended right in with the common people so much so that even His powerful miracles weren't enough to convince those waiting for a different looking

Messiah. Jesus was considered uneducated by the Sanhedrin, which was the governing body of religious rulers. He did not live up to their qualifying standards of the day.

Something really appeals to me knowing that. Jesus said He wasn't doing things on His own. He did His Father's works through the power of the Holy Spirit, as will we when we are led by God's Spirit, taking what belongs to Jesus to give to others. This is His will.

If we are God's vessels—as Word-bearers—we may be ordinary, yet our works will be, in reality, God's works. What an incredible thing to partner with the Creator.

My daughter and her husband recently had a baby. They made a beautiful baby boy. He is precious and wonderful. But, they can't take the credit for creating this person any more than a writer can for writing things inspired by God. So, we can relax. It's a collaboration.

Sherwood Wirt's *Writing to Inspire* greatly influenced me to want to take my prayer and writing experiences and allow them to be used by God for others. The following are notes and quotes I gleaned from his book. I've italicized direct quotes.

> *We are scribes in the Temple if we are writing for Jesus. How do you know if you are called to be one? Do you want to? Is it more than a want? Is it a must? C.S. Lewis said 'writing is a lust; it is "scratching where you itch."'*

> *"And I guess that many of us would confess that we write simply because we have to. We're 'word' people, and if we cannot preach like Peter or pray like Paul, at least we can write like the devil."*

Let's be God's messengers. Jesus said we would do the works He did and even greater works. We have no record of anything Jesus might have written. Yet, Scripture is made up of His inspired words. That is why we must believe that He speaks to and through us, too.

*O*ur reason for writing is also 'whose' we are. Truth is we are on the battlefield for the Lord. There are so many 'causes'—we need to hear our own marching orders. Really, it's not a matter of what we do—but who we are. Words like salt and light should describe us. Look around at our world. In these evil days, darker than ever before, we can be the light that pierces the darkness. Inspirational writers can permeate this culture—just as in the past." - Sherwood Wirt.

These days we write for screens as well as the printed page. We have amazing media at our disposal. The Internet. Blogs. E-Books. Screenwriting. Audio books. Online streaming. Email. Electronic self-publishing. Think about the tools and resources we have available to us. This *Information Age* we've found ourselves in is part of God's larger story—we are the characters in God's "reality drama"—and this time was predicted in Scripture to usher in the last of the Last Days.

Are we the ones to do it? God gave us life and put us here and wants to inspire us to inspire others—to write from the fire within.

*C*hristian writers believe that Jesus, who gives meaning to everything in life, gives meaning and purpose to their writing. Religious and inspired writing is not in the mainstream of today's literature. Would that it was! That is something we should strive for. We should strive for excellence in the art."

-Sherwood Wirt

We know well that the world loves the darkness and shuns the light. Have you noticed that the books most popular in our generation are filled with darkness—immoral and flagrant sex, violence, horror, crime, bloodshed, because the world is filled with soiled, depraved minds and hearts. How Satan has stolen God's children, removing them far from the beauty and good God intends for us.

Remember, being an artist, in this case, writing, means we are to be a bearer of the Word—like Mary. "Be it done to me according to your word."

There is such power and permanence with the written word. When Paul preached the Gospel of Jesus in his own day, there was another favorite teacher at the time who was having a meaningful impact on the same churches. His name was Apollos. It is believed that Apollos was a better orator than Paul, much better, in fact. Paul admitted he wasn't that much of a skilled orator/preacher—but he could really write. His letters to the churches transformed the world. They affect us today in ways that we cannot begin to appreciate. Today no one knows what Apollos had to say.

Many major movements in recorded history have been brought about through literature. Most writers are convinced not only of the power of the written page but also of its permanence. Today in our local libraries we can, just by asking, or through internet search engines, just by clicking, read the ideas of innumerable great thinkers and world-changers. We can even read ancient literature that has been preserved. You never know who will read what we write—now, or in the future.

A testimony . . .

About twenty-five years ago, while hearing a sermon series in church, I was convinced the messages needed to get out to the Church at large and to the world. Our senior pastor was teaching about "the pain of porneia." Porneia is Latin and means sexual immorality. His teaching was graceful, full of God's love. They were healing messages that oozed with God's wisdom, as well as eye-opening prediction. This was a clear, bright light the pastor preached and timely.

The world was quickly changing in matters of sexual morality and the church was beginning to be compromised too. The disintegration of marriage, emotional and sexual abuse in families, premarital sex viewed as preferred conduct, growing divorce rates, and a general degradation of moral values everywhere, all of this, and more, was rapidly changing our society and culture—including believers. Here was a voice for God warning of the impending sway of accepted tolerance preparing the Church for the onslaught.

I felt God urging me to help see that the series of teachings get published. I decided to volunteer my time to type out the sixteen sermon messages. Dictaphone transcription was the task I would take on. At the time, the tide was turning, and Christians needed to be warned of how our society was quickly down-spiraling and to be aware of God's concern.

Before I had a chance to tell anyone about my idea, I went to an early prayer meeting. It was about 6:00 A.M., very unusual for me to be up, and still dark. It had been snowing heavily for a couple of hours, a typical Minnesota wintry morning. When I pulled into the parking lot, I noticed only one other car parked there. Fresh footprints led away from it to a side door in the building. I followed the footprints because I'd never been to the administrative offices and I wasn't sure where to find an unlocked door so early in the morning. The church gathered on weekends in a large school auditorium that was not close by but prayer meetings and administration happened in this building.

As I followed the footprints in the snow, the Lord spoke within me, "These footprints will melt away soon. His tracks need to be made lasting."

I was surprised by these thoughts. I had no idea whose footprints they were. When I entered the building I found that they belonged to the pastor. He had wanted to stop in to pick something up. I had never met him in person because it was a church of thousands and I was a new member. So, there in the early morning quiet, I introduced myself and explained the idea I had regarding his sermon series. After several meetings with the publishing department, it was agreed that it was definitely something God wanted. His message needed permanence. How rewarding and exciting to be part of God's important and timely work. The Book of Acts is still being written.

Think about the moral decay of our culture, the continual down-spiraling of our society worldwide. The overwhelming amount of filthy jokes and humor belongs in the gutter. We are witnessing utter disintegration of values, the landslide abandonment of taboos in our society.

We swim against a muddy flood. But we can draw our inspiration from a clear stream that has come down through the centuries—from Paul, Augustine, Francis, Lady Julian, Thomas a' Kempis, Luther, Madame Guyon, Bunyan, Oswald Chambers, Amy Carmichael." -Sherwood Wirt.

We have newer voices, including Sherwood Wirt himself, Billy Graham and Anne Graham Lotz, Francis Schaeffer, Brennan Manning, John Eldridge, Dallas Willard, Richard Foster, Mike Bickle, Max Lucado, Madeleine L'Engle, Joel Rosenberg, and so many more. My pastor, Steven Furtick, in Charlotte, is writing New York Times bestsellers for God.

Before we know it, it will be future generations' turn to speak for God. For now, we have big shoes to fill: Sherwood Wirt, Francis Schaeffer, Brennan Manning, Dallas Willard, and Madeleine L'Engle, all these gifted messengers in my lifetime are now in Heaven—many I've quoted in this book.

The Christian writer takes to her/his typewriter because God in His sovereign grace has stooped down and lighted his candle. No longer is he his own or she her own woman. Their lives have been claimed; they are now the occupied territory of the Holy Spirit. The prophet Habakkuk's orders were: 'Write the vision and make it plain, that he may run who reads.' -Sherwood Wirt.

When we experience an on-going close relationship with God, we will be inspired as we write. What many writers often call "serendipity," I like to call "inspired," in that characters and subplots appear and weave together almost with a life of their own, often surprising the writer during the process.

For example, a character suddenly appears in the process of writing a story. You didn't plan for him but there he is. This happened to me while writing the novel on the life of Jesus. When I first set out to write that book, my desire was to recreate the Gospel narratives into a "novel" approach. I wanted to give description and probable chronology with believable scenes, but I had intended to stay strictly to the Gospel narratives. I did not plan to add fictional characters. It unsettled me at first when the first ones began popping up while writing the first draft. I was five chapters in with an unwanted fictional character, a small part at the time, but it bothered me.

I sent my work to a friend, a Christian writer and editor, for her opinion. She advised me to allow the characters to come. This completely changed the style of the book. As it turned out, a few others arrived, and the first unwanted character had a small part that grew. He ended up a main character, a Jerusalem scribe of the Sanhedrin, carrying a major theme and tool for teaching in the sequel book. God knew what He had planned for that character in the beginning. At the time, I never imagined writing a second novel about the primitive church in Jerusalem. In the beginning, I needed to be "obedient" to the work because it is a vital writing dynamic for Christian writers who want their work to be inspired. I thank Madeleine L'Engle's book, *Walking on Water: Reflections on Faith and Art* for her expert guidance. Here is another example of how our relationship with God, faith, prayer, and inspiration comes to us as grace.

A testimony . . .

While writing *God in Sandals*, the novel I described above, I used a harmony of the Gospels for my story outline. I had come to the time in Jesus' life just after angels had ministered to Him in the wilderness. It followed His forty-day fast and temptation. My next scene would be to describe Jesus rejoining John the Baptist at the Jordan River because Jesus returned there next. I had intended to include the occasion when John and Andrew first met Jesus and spent the day with Him—which marked the beginning of Jesus' public ministry.

I was about to start typing on my keyboard when I sensed the Lord ask me to sit quietly and not write anything yet. The fact I felt God speaking to me first-person while writing was not the norm and I felt surprised and excited about it. I obeyed the Lord. I sat still and didn't think about anything, I was simply aware of God's presence. Suddenly, an amazing vision came to me. It turned out to become the basis for my next scene in which I described Jesus waking from a dream at the place where He had just been refreshed by angels at a waterfall and small natural pool in the Judean wilderness. It's a real place called En Gedi.

It was my vision from the Holy Spirit that influenced me on what I would write concerning Jesus' experience there. He awakens from a dream and my scene is His recollection of it. In other words, He "relives" His dream. It's not a scene in the Harmony of the Gospels. However, because of my "stillness" time, I saw what was described in the book of Revelation as Jesus' triumphal coming, King Jesus in great glory, the Messiah riding a white horse, arriving at the Mount of Olives and then proceeding to Jerusalem's East Gate to be welcomed by representatives of Israel. He had come along with a cloud of witnesses, a great multitude riding horses in the heavens.

They were from diverse peoples and nations and they carried banners and praised Him. I saw Jesus in vivid detail, the ends of His sash were red, having been dipped in blood, and His earthly disciples (Peter, John, James, etc.) were close to Him. After He dismounts from His horse on the summit of the Mount of Olives, the two mountains split, Mount Moriah and the Mount of Olives, opening the East Gate, which had been blocked shut (another real prophecy).

He and His disciples remount and ride toward the now open East (Golden) Gate. Just after Jesus passes through the prophetic gate in Jesus' dream (that is, my vision of it), it ends with a surprise. Instead of dismounting from the white horse inside Jerusalem's East Gate, Jesus finds Himself dismounting from the colt of a donkey. Just when Israel is about to recognize Him as having been Jesus of Nazareth, the One they rejected, He is back to being Jesus of Nazareth—the humble one—the Son of Man—the One not recognized or believed in by Israel's rulers.

In my story's scene, Jesus acknowledges with deep understanding and commitment that His public life as the Messiah is about to begin and it is time to be the humble, servant-Messiah. It seemed so poignant to me that Jesus, in my fictional story, saw ahead and compared the contrasting experiences as Messiah, both prophesied in the Scriptures to happen at the East Gate. I would never have thought of such a scene if I hadn't felt guided by the Lord to be quiet because He had something special to inspire for the next scene. I don't think it would have come during free-writing because I was sticking close to the outline. Whether or not Jesus had such a dream, I don't know. However, I received an amazing vision and was able to teach an important aspect, a heart-to-heart insight, about Jesus' life, through the creative art of storytelling.

Inspired, Effective Writing Comes To You. First, write what God has inspired in you. Write from the fire within. You must not use any voice but your own or readers will know you are faking. Write something you'd love to read because then you will write something effective. Get what's inside your heart onto the page. You must be authentic, brave, and open. You must like it yourself or no one else will like it. As a writer, I fail, not when a reader is not moved, but when I, as a reader, am not moved.

I looked for months for a certain kind of book and couldn't find it. If there's a book you want to read, but it hasn't been written yet, then you must write it. All the years of meditative prayer came to life, flowing with inspired authenticity because of the fire within. I've been told *God in Sandals* portrays Jesus as human, close and touchable, while undiminished in divinity. I broke literary "rules" in that the point of view jumps around. I also wrote a fictionalized account of Jesus, which Christian publishers are not excited to do. But I obeyed the work that came to me. Then, miracle of all miracles, it was later published as an audio book by a top audio publisher in the secular industry. You just never know what prayer and writing might do. And, as an audio book, the writing works well as a listening experience.

Find out the reason you want to write. Is it because the desire is deep down in your heart? How would you feel if you were forbidden to write it?

> *A*ll we have to decide is what to do with the time that is *given to us." AND "To thine own self be true."*
>
> - William Shakespeare

Think about your experiences and how you've changed and grown from reading. We need to write from the inside out.

Here are some practical guidelines:

1. **Pray & Be Available, Open to God.** Be a person in communion with God. Discipline. Make prayer and writing a habit. Listen.

Listen to God and to your life. Notice. Reflect. Meditate. Study. Waste time *be*-ing—if you do not do enough of this you will be too busy to become creative. Absorb. Give silence a chance to fill you with God's wisdom. Much of it comes when we are resting or silent. Be still within often in order to receive the creative Word. Practice being aware of God's presence, able to receive the Lord's whispers and nudges.

2. **Guard Your Words.** Be accountable for them; they are powerful.

3. **Be Obedient** to God's desires in you. Realize that, as a writer, you are called to be a gentle healer and teacher following Jesus of Nazareth.

4. **Keep Pure Motives.**

We are surrounded by the ravages of sin and suffering, like Jesus was, and we cannot ignore it. We want to take hold of one small corner of human burden and lift, together with anyone else who will join us. If we had to choose between swabbing the dirty floors of a nursing home and writing a brilliant essay that would win international acclaim but helped nobody, we would swab the floor!" - Sherwood Wirt

When Writing Becomes Your Ministry and Your "Yes" to God. Begin where you are. Write from your relationship with God. You could start by writing letters to your loved ones. What about inspirational blogs? What could you share with friends, a church group, or your family? God will show you. Or, for those who burn to be published—usually that "burning" is a call from God. Listen to your passions, if they are good ones, that is where God usually is. How wonderful that the Lord gives us the desires of our hearts. He puts the desires in us to act and do according to His pleasure—and our own.

I hope the following notes from Sherwood Wirt's *Writing to Inspire* will be the kindling, along with God's breath blown in, that will ignite your writing fire so that sparks will fly out from your fire and set other fires elsewhere. (Quotations from his book are italicized.)

Instead of thinking of our own footsteps as being lost in the

sands of time, we can leave something infinitely better:

a word fitly spoken—writing what might influence a life or even

save a generation

writing that wants to make things happen

writing that will sway opinion and change lives

action literature designed to rouse people from their sleep

like Jesus did through

precepts, admonition,

example, parable, poem

and every known literary device—so that

men and women may be informed of their opportunities,

inspired by their Lord and

warned of their peril.

We are commissioned to teach

train

interpret

inform

edify

narrate stories as Jesus did

mend and heal

encourage

be peacemakers

lead into truth

unite and bind up

free and enlighten

comfort

bring laughter

challenge lies

Milk for children—solid food for adults—the elixir of poetry to express our love for our Creator.

Write about good and evil . . . frustration and victory . . . justice and mercy, sin and redemption . . . joy and adversity . . . grace and glory.

In this day we live in we need to pierce the darkness and prepare the coming of the Lord. We need the spirit of Elijah and John the Baptist. We need to be aware of the times and what God wants us to do.

Be Sensitive to God, Our times, and Write What You *Want* to Write. Think about the age we live in and how many people are alive on the earth. We could be very near the Lord's glorious, historic climax. His Story's climax. Who are the movers God is using today? Where is God in your own life? This is the material from which to draw. Have you ever noticed this phrase in Luke 1:1-4? (Note the capitalized words.)

Inasmuch as many have taken in hand to set in order a narrative of those things which have been fulfilled among us, just as those who from the beginning were eyewitnesses and ministers of the word delivered them to us, IT SEEMED GOOD TO ME also, having had perfect understanding of all things from the very first, TO WRITE TO YOU AN ORDERLY ACCOUNT, most excellent Theophilus, that you may know the certainty of those things in which you were instructed."

Luke never knew God meant to turn his writing into Scripture, part of the God-breathed-Word that would profoundly affect the world over the history of the Church. No, it seemed good to him to write his friend an "orderly account." You never know how God will use what you write. We only need to do what is in our hearts to do—do what seems good to you. It could be much more than you'll ever know this side of Heaven.

Begin where you are. It usually takes 5 to 10 years for a motivated person who works at it, seeks and learns the rules and nuances of the field, to get published by a traditional publisher. Or, you can self-publish. These are amazing times full of opportunity for us. We can easily write to inspire because of the tools, resources, and opportunities we have at our disposal. We are living in an age of grace and enlightenment because Jesus is returning soon.

You need good contacts and disciplines (habits). Remember, God is with you and writing is an art and craft; it takes practice and it is a process, like anything else. Above all, write from your heart and life.

♋ Prayer Journal Exercise for Session Four

Our inner life and our prayer will be the oil that fuels our writing. Here is a Scripture quotation to ponder and own. Write your prayerful thoughts in your prayer journal. What is your particular "gift" God has given to you that would help or inspire others? What is God saying to you at this moment regarding this powerful truth?

I. From 1 Corinthians 1:27, according to Apostle Paul:

G od chose those whom the world considers absurd to shame the wise; He singled out the weak of this world to shame the strong."

II. A Scripture Verse Study and Writing Exercise:

1. Choose a Scripture verse.
2. Underline or highlight the key words.
3. Look up the key words in a dictionary or thesaurus.
4. Paraphrase the verse using the information you gained from the definitions.
5. Read the verse in the context of the Scripture. How does the context help you understand the meaning of the verse?
6. Personalize it. This could be an active word from God.

Suggested verses:

Ps. 23 (Good Shepherd); Ps. 45 (God's loves); Lk. 13:24 (narrow gate); Is. 42:16 (God leads); Is. 43:1-2 (God redeems); Is. 43:18-19 (God does a new thing); Deut. 6:4—5 (the Shema/Hear, O Israel); Phil. 1:6 (running the race); Eph. 4:15 (express truth & love); Eph. 3:20 (above all we ask or hope); Is. 53 (Messiah's suffering); Ps. 90:14 (see the following example); Ps. 68:19 (Praising God); Ps. 66:20 (God is with me); Ps. 22 (to deepen one's understanding of the suffering of Jesus on the cross); Matt. 22:44 & Ps. 110:1 (Son of David is the Lord of David).

Example:

Psalm 90:17: "May the favor of the Lord our God rest upon us; establish the work of our hands for us—yes, establish the work of our hands."

I underlined the KEY words as shown above and looked them up in the dictionary:

"favor" – courtesy, kindness, service, approval, blessing, approbation, commendation

"God" – Sovereign Creator

"rest" – gently linger, pause, stop, tarry

"upon" – on

"establish" – authenticate, confirm, prove, validate, verify

"work" – job, labor, toil, chore, occupation, employment

"hand(s)" – fist, palm, employee, laborer, worker, workman, applause, handwriting, penmanship, script, writing

Next, I interpret, according to the above meanings while listening to what God stirs within my heart for me to expound on.

Result: "May the kindness and blessing and service of the Lord our sovereign Creator, gently linger and tarry upon us; proving and validating our labor for us, yes, confirming and verifying the labor and toil of our writing."

The take-away: God is "yes" toward what is good for me and is proving and affirming my labor as a writer.

SESSION FIVE

SHARING WITH OTHERS

⊂ঃ Insructions

If you are participating in this workshop physically with a group, allow at least one-hour to one-and-a-half-hours to do both parts of Session Five. Divide into smaller groups of 3 to 6 people if your total participants are more than 6 people. If you stay in larger groups, you may not have enough time plus people tend to share more easily and openly if in a smaller, more intimate group.

By sharing prayer and writing experiences with others, it seems to affirm and bring more permanence and reality to the experience for the person who does the sharing as well as those who are listening. As a result, your group's sharing time becomes more experience of God for everyone present.

For individuals, please continue with Session Five's prayer exercises. You may want to share your experiences with others in whatever way the Lord leads you. Ideally, you will find a place or a way to share your inspired writing with others while the fire still burns within you. Remember this quote by David Thoreau at the beginning of this book:

> W*rite while the heat is in you. The writer who postpones the recording of his thoughts uses an iron which has cooled to burn a hole with. He cannot inflame the minds of his audience."*

Part 1 of Session 5

∞ Prayer & Writing Exercise for Session Five

The goal in this time is to see what comes while you listen, reflect, and write. Begin in silence for three to five minutes being present to God. It takes time to quiet the thoughts and noise in our minds.

Next, choose one of these Scriptures that seems to stir or invite you to ponder further.

Psalm 84:5
"Blessed is the man whose strength is in You,
Whose heart is set on pilgrimage."

Psalm 89:15
"Blessed are the people who know the joyful sound!
They walk, O Lord, in the light of Your countenance."

Psalm 45:1
"My heart is overflowing with a good theme;
I recite my composition concerning the King:
My tongue is the pen of a ready writer."

You could turn that around to

"My pen is a ready speaker of Your mouth."

Luke 8:45
"Who touched Me?"

Luke 9:20
"Who do you say I am?"
Or, more personally,
Jesus asks you in this prayer time, *"Who am I to you?"*

Song of Solomon 5:2
"I sleep, but my heart is awake; it is the voice of my beloved!"

Song of Solomon 5:6b
"My heart leaped when He spoke."

Song of Solomon 4:9
"You have ravished My heart, My sister, My bride . . ."

After choosing your Scripture or its theme, ask the Lord to inspire you and then please begin. Write whatever flows. Sometimes using other words to rewrite the verse gets you started. As you have thoughts or ideas coming, write them down. This can be anything or in any form. This is prayerful free-writing, without caring about grammar or spelling or finding perfect words. Just write what comes to you for 10 minutes or so.

Spend another 15 minutes rewriting it, if you want. Rewriting may bring in new writing; you build on it. You are in God's presence communing with Him, one with His Spirit, being inspired (breathed into) by God. During the actual process of writing, we can learn or receive insight as we put words down. This is the time to be receptive to whatever the Holy Spirit wants to impart.

Part 2 of Session 5

cs Group Sharing for Session Five

Please note that this is the second-half of Session Five, meant for group sharing. You'll need designated group facilitators. For the sake of time, participants should pick one of the six primers for discussion. Use these suggestions as a way to share with one another.

It works best if everyone takes about five minutes to read the list and choose which number they want to share. Then limit the individual sharing times according to how many people are in your group. Break down into discussion groups of no more than six participants per group. It's always powerful to end the day with prayer for one another, asking God for personal blessing and directon for everyone.

1. From the teaching—What inspired, encouraged, or spoke to you that seemed significant?

2. From the meditations and reflections—How did God reveal Himself to you when you imagined a Gospel scene? Can you share with others what this was like for you? What did you see, hear, feel, learn? What was your most significant take-away?

3. What was your journaling experience like? Did you receive anything from the Lord you would like to share? Did you learn anything, or were you touched or ministered to by God?

4. From writing as a way of ministry—Do you want to share a piece of writing that came from your "Moving Outward: Writing to inspire?" This would be from our last prayer and writing exercise.

5. Any questions or comments you would like to discuss about the sessions or the workshop experience in general?

CREDITS

1. *Prayer: Finding the Heart's True Home*, Richard J. Foster, ©HarperOne/HarperCollins, 1992. Foster's teaching on the three movements of prayer inspired the idea for the prayer and writing sessions for this book.

2. *Walking on Water: Reflections of Faith and Art*, Madeleine L'Engle, ©Crosswicks 1980, Waterbrook Multnomah.

3. *Communion With God*, ©Mark Virkler, Buffalo School of the Bible, out of print.

4. *Your Move God by* ©Francis Clare, New Leaf Press, 1982.

5. *Jesus Calling* by Sarah Young, Copyright © 2004 by Sarah Young, Used by permission of Thomas Nelson. www.thomasnelson.com.

6. *Writing to Inspire*, ©Sherwood Wirt, out of print.

Love's Face

An inspirational book about Jesus as the Lover of the soul.

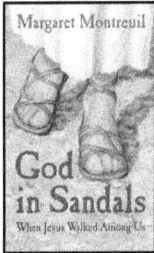

God in Sandals

A biblical novel on the life of Jesus. *(Also in audio book format.)*

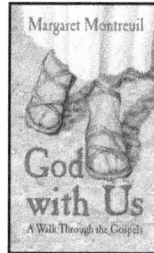

God with Us

Inspirational stand-alone book on Jesus' life & companion to *God in Sandals*.

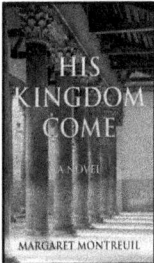

His Kingdom Come

A biblically-based novel about the primitive Church in Jerusalem. Sequel to *God in Sandals*.

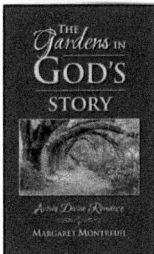

The Gardens in God's Story

An inspirational book about Divine Romance.

Available to order in any book store.

Visit www.margaretmontreuil.com for book synopses and excerpts, upcoming projects-in-process, and more information.